Serial Killers

Most Horrific Serial Killers Biographies, True Crime Cases, Murderers

monetary loss due to the information herein, either directly or indirectly.

Introduction

I want to thank you and congratulate you for purchasing the book, *"Serial Killers - Most Horrific Serial Killers Biographies, True Crime Cases, Murderers"*.

It is not in the natural wiring of a man (or woman) to take another man's life. It is even more unnatural when the person has a compulsion to keep taking lives, so that he satisfies some twisted craving. The psychology of serial killers is a bit difficult to explore. The reason is that it is not something that is set in rigid boundaries. It appears that after every murder, an extra layer is added to it. It also appears that the humane side of a serial killer dies a little more with every killing.

Do you want to learn more about serial killers? Are you interested in knowing what led them down that path? If you do, this book does a great job of looking at what drove the different people to serial killers. It is important to note that nothing justifies taking life but rather we try to look at what made sense in the eyes of the serial killer to do what they did and with no remorse for their actions.

Thanks again for purchasing this book, I hope you enjoy it!

Table of Contents

Donald "Pee Wee" Henry Gaskins: The Killer Who Killed Hitchhikers

Who Was Donald Henry Gaskins

"Pee Wee" Gaskins claimed that he had murdered between 80 and 90 people. He killed them by torturing and then mutilating them, in that order. He picked up the habit of picking up hitchhikers on American South's coastal highways and torturing them to death. It was not until a criminal associate snitched on him after he saw him kill two young men that he was arrested. Initially, the judge sentenced him to death but this was later overturned to life imprisonment without any chance of parole. While still on death row, Gaskins added another murder to his resume. He thus became the only man in history to have killed a man while on death row.

Early life

Gaskins was born in 1933 in the county of Florence, South Carolina. He was the last child of the illegitimate children his mother, Eulea Parrott had. He was small, leading to his peers giving him the nickname "Pee Wee". In addition to this, he was constantly bullied and teased. However, the bigger problem for Gaskins may have been at home. His mother did not really care much about him and his different stepfathers beat him regularly.

It appears that the constant teasing and fighting in school wore Gaskins' out. At age 11 he dropped out and begun working on automobiles, which must have made a lot of sense given the obsession that boys have with cars. While working in the garage, he met two lads, Marsh and Danny. The similarities between them drew them to each other. They were not only the same age, but they were also out of school. They teamed up and formed "The Trouble Trio", a gang of three with a penchant for burglarizing homes, raping little boys and picking up prostitutes. Gaskins and his pals understood that they stood a high chance of getting in trouble with the police on account of the little boys they violated. To minimize the risk, they used threats on them.

One day, the trio decided to gang rape Marsh's small sister. The trouble was that Marsh's parents were around, and they caught them in the act. Their punishment was that they were whipped until they bled. Danny and Marsh left the area a short while after that but Gaskins remained and continued to rob homes on his own.

The first trial

A girl who knew Gaskins interrupted him one day as he attempted to burglarize her home. She struck him with an axe but he managed to wrench it from her and strike her on the head with it. She survived and thus, got Gaskins arrested and convicted for assault.

Release from prison, his first hitchhiker murder, and the coastal kills

Henry Gaskins, after his release from prison, was arrested for raping a twelve-year-old girl. He absconded but was rearrested in Georgia. He was sentenced to 8 years in prison. He was paroled in November of 1968.

Gaskins' first hitchhiker killing was in September 1969. He tortured and murdered a woman before dumping her body in a swamp.

The hitchhiker was one of many that he would kill. He killed at least once every 6 weeks, and called them "coastal kills". He tortured and mutilated his victims, all the while trying to ensure that they remained alive for as long as possible to meet his need for violence. He confessed to killing about 90 or so victims.

Gaskins was arrested on November the 14th 1975 when a criminal associate confessed he had seen Gaskins kill Dennis Bellamy, 28 and Johnny Knight, 15.

Execution

Gaskins was executed on September 6, 1991. He was the 4th person to die on the electric chair, after the death penalty was reinstated in South Carolina in 1977. His last words were, "I'll let the lawyers talk for me. I'm ready to go."

A Psychological Analysis of Gaskins

Gaskins grew up knowing little except violence. It is easy to see how the violence was compounded in Gaskins' young brain.

Violence at school

For starters, he leaves school after endless teasing and scuffles. His major reason for leaving school is violence.

Violence at home

Usually, bullied kids find relief at home. This is however not the case with Gaskins. He simply moves from one violent place to another. His stepfathers beat him regularly.

A different kind of violence on the street (From being the prey to being the predator)

Gaskins gets the understanding that there is more to be gained from dictating the terms of violence as opposed to reacting to violent situations. Therefore, instead of learning from the violence and understanding the pain he went through because of the violence, he becomes violent himself. He burglarizes houses and rapes little boys and in order to ensure the boys don't report the case to the police, they threaten them.

Gaskins' gang rape incident and the violent punishment that follows

Gaskins is punished violently, further compounding the idea that violence is THE way of life. Watch his reaction though, in contrast to his friends'. Rather than back off, he insists on following the path of violence. This works to reinforce the belief in him that the only way to live is to bleed.

Gaskins strikes girl on the skull with an axe

Gaskins reacts in the only way he knows how, when he feels threatened. He wrenches the axe from the girl's hand and hits her on the head. His first instinct is to react with violence. At this point, violence has taken center stage in his life.

Gaskins' first court trial

What crosses your mind once someone uses your name? The standard feeling is one of respect and appreciation. Gaskins feels the "odd" feelings of appreciation and respect in a court of law as he is convicted for various crimes. It makes sense to assume that this stokes the fire within him to continue down the same path. If that is the only way for him to get "appreciated and respected", why not continue on the same path? If this looks like immature rationalization to you, then understand that Gaskins was immature at this point. Even the courts could not jail him since he was only fourteen years old. Thus, he was sent to reform school.

Gaskins, after his conviction

At reform school, Gaskins was immediately a target for bullying, owing to his small stature. He was attacked and raped. To protect himself, Gaskins had to resort to protection from the "Boss Boy". The currency was sex.

After his release, Gaskins splits a girl's skull with a hammer after she asks him questions about arsons he was suspected of. Actually, he was guilty of them. Gaskins gets a five-year sentence for assault and attempted murder.

In order to become a "power man" in prison, he commits his first murder. He is sentenced to 6 months in solitary, but acquires his power man status just the same. He uses violence to escape violence. He is thrown into solitary for six months, an unfriendly environment, only to be thrust back into the violent prison ranks.

After he is convicted again for rape and being sentenced to 8 years, he kills yet another inmate. He is later released from prison and kills his first hitchhiker, who was a woman. This sets the pace for more murders. Back in prison, he kills yet again. His very existence is one continuous thread of violence

What do we learn

Gaskins was introduced to violence at a very tender age. First, owing to his small frame, he is the brunt of attacks. He reacts, naturally, because he needs to protect himself and his ego but he continues to become more violent even when he is not teased. Therefore, we can conclude that from a young age, Gaskins was conditioned to believe that violence was life, something he adhered to sustain even when the reasons for being violent were simply, for the sake of it.

Paul John Knowles: The Casanova Killer

Paul John Knowles, Who Was He

A native of Florida, born in 1946, Knowles father gave him up to live in foster homes after he committed a petty crime. John Knowles was first arrested at the age of 19. Thereafter, he spent at least half of every year that followed in jail, on various convictions of car theft and burglary. He was spending jail time in Raiford when he made correspondence with Angela Covic. Miss Covic was a divorcee. She visited prison long enough for him to propose to her. She provided the money he needed to hire lawyers who would lobby for his parole. However, after a visit to a psychic who warned her against marrying "a new dangerous man in her life", she dumped him just as he was being released. On that night that he was dumped, he confessed to killing three people.

After his rejection by Angela, Knowles was highly agitated, and this is what spurred him to spree killing. He went on a killing spree across Northern Maine. He killed at least 18 people, though he estimated the total number to be 35.

Victims, in order

Alice Cooper: She was a 65 year old woman who lived in Jacksonville, Florida. She was gagged by Knowles on July 26, 1974, as he burglarized her home. She choked to death on the gag.

Lillian and Mylette Anderson: They were little girls aged eleven and seven. After stealing Alice Cooper's car, he drove it around town for a while before deciding to dump it on a quiet street. He however came across both girls and knew that they recognized him (their family was friends with his). He killed them by strangulation to prevent them from giving him away. He dumped their bodies in a nearby swamp.

Marjorie Howe: He strangled her with a nylon stocking. His motive was to steal her T.V set.

Victim #5: She remains anonymous. All that is known of her is that she was a hitchhiker whom Knowles raped and strangled to get a "fix".

Kathy Pierce: He strangled her using a telephone cord. However, he did not harm her 3-year-old son, who watched the whole thing.

William Bates: He was a businessman whom Knowles charmed and had a few drinks with. He was killed by Knowles on September 3 and his corpse was not discovered until October. Knowles took his car and some money.

Emmett and Lois Johnson: They were camping in Nevada. Knowles walked up to them as though he was a friendly man, before murdering them. This was on September 18, 1974.

Victim #10: She was a woman on a motorcycle. When it broke down, Knowles stopped as though to help, before strangling her and dragging her corpse through barbed wire.

Ann Dawson: Ann Dawson was a beautician who was smitten by his "gaunt good looks" and charisma. They travelled together for some time, from September 23, before he got tired of her and killed her on the 29th. Her corpse was never found.

Doris Harvey: She was a 53 year old woman in Virginia. Knowles shot her dead with her husband's rifle before laying it by her side.

Carswell Carr and his daughter: Carr met the charming Knowles on November the 6th in Macon, and invited him over. Knowles then stabbed her dead before strangling his daughter. He tried to rape her corpse.

Edward Hilliard and Debbie Griffin: They were hitchhikers near Macon. Hilliard's body was found in woods nearby but Debbie's were never found.

Trooper Charles Campell: While on patrol, he attempted to stop Knowles. Knowles was faster to the draw, and abducted him, using his cruiser to escape. He was handcuffed to a tree and shot.

James Meyer: He was a businessman who Knowles took hostage along with Trooper Campbell. He met his fate in the same manner, by being handcuffed to a tree and shot in the head at close range.

A Psychological Analysis

Knowles was introduced to the prison system at the age of 19. He seems to have suffered an intense compulsion to commit crimes, which is why he spent so much of his lifetime in jail. He was also a real charmer, which made it possible for him to seduce Angela Covic.

Agitation at rejection

Angela Covic dumping him is what started it all; what made him to become a serial killer from an auto thief. After being dumped, he becaem highly agitated, killing three people that night and he keeps his spree killing for the rest of the month. Knowles initially, while a criminal, was not a serial killer. However, his rejection opened a festering ulcer within that compelled him to "exert revenge". This may be explained this way: as a naturally charming man, he is not used to people refusing his advances and being dumped. Angela dumping him makes him feel like he is in unfamiliar territory. Therefore, in an attempt to get that power back, he seeks to kill.

Angela dumping him also made him hate women greatly. Only about five of his victims were men. Now, two of those were in the company of women, so he may have had to kill them anyway to get rid of witnesses. Of the other three, one was a trooper who was trying to arrest him and the other two were businessmen whom he needed to rob. This clearly shows that John had a great dislike for women and a compulsion to kill them owing to the heartbreak.

So, why was he able to kill many women as well as men? Knowles was a good-looking man with effortless charisma. He was able to use this charm on both women and men alike, charming them into dropping their guard down before killing them. To understand his extraordinary charm, realize that almost all of Knowles' murders are concentrated in the month of September alone. He was able to seduce so many people and kill them in the space of a month.

Tsutomu Miyazaki, The Murderer Of Little Girls

Who Was Tsutomu Miyazaki?

Early life

Tsutomu was born prematurely in 1962 to a wealthy family. Owing to his premature birth, he had deformed hands that gnarled and fused directly with the wrists meaning that in order to rotate his hand; he had to move his entire forearm. This made him the target of ridicule in Itsukaichi Elementary School. This was compounded by his parents who seemed to involved in their work. His father concentrated so much on his business and collecting cameras while her mother spent most of her time at work and in order to address her own guilt on not spending time with her son, he bought her gifts. This in addition to ridicule in school led him to keep to himself. He immersed himself in the world of comic and fantasy. According to a classmate in high school, Tsutomu had a small penis and combining this with his deformity, he thought no one would be attracted to him. Therefore, he would take his camera and photography his classmates as they played tennis in short dresses, and then he would later masturbate with using the videos.

In addition, we can assume his need for child pornography was fuelled by the thought that he could not attract any women owing to his small penis that a classmate referred to as, "not wider than a pencil and not longer than a toothpick". Therefore, child pornography was a release for Tsutomu.

His killings

Tsutomu's first victim was a girl called Konno Mari. She was only four years old. He lured her into his car and after killing her, raped her corpse. He allowed her to decompose for a little while and then burned her bones in a furnace. However, he preserved her hands and feet. He sent the rest of her remains to the girl's family with a postcard that read "Mari, cremated, bones, Investigate".

Victim no. 2, 3 & 4

Tsutomu's second victim, Masami, was killed in the same way. This time round, he took her clothes with him as a trophy. As for his third victim, a four year old called Namba Erika, he took pictures of her while she was still alive before killing her and dumping her body. However, he retained her clothes as souvenirs. He sent the family a postcard with cutouts of the words "Erika, Cold, Cough, Throat, Death".

The fourth victim and the fifth failed one

Tsutomu killed his fourth victim, filmed himself sexually assaulting her corpse and then dismembered her. He dumped the head and body miles apart but brought them back to his house a few weeks later and stashed them in his closet. Before dumping, he put her hands away, eating a part of them.

Tsutomu was caught when his attempts to capture his fifth victim were interrupted by her father. He escaped on foot but when he came back for his car, he was arrested.

The trial & execution

Throughout his trial, he was calm and indifferent. His words were "There is not much I can say about them, other than I did a good deed. At least that is what I did."

His father committed suicide over his gruesome deeds. On learning of this, Tsutomu's words were "I feel refreshed".

Tsutomu's last words before his 2008 execution were, "Please tell the world that I am a gentleman."

A Psychological Analysis
Tsutomu's addiction to child pornography

One of the things that pornography does is trigger the release of large doses of endorphin in the brain. This is similar to exercising. The difference is that rather than achieve that state of calm that follows from working muscle to exhaustion, the brain is conditioned to ask for more. Take the example of how cocaine addiction works in people, to understand this better. Thus, you feel compelled to view more of the same. If the fetish lies in watching cruel scenes, you can only sate yourself by watching them. If child pornography is your thing, the same is the case. With time, your dose of pornographic scenes becomes too normalized, and you seek out increasingly brutal scenes. It is likely that you will get to a point where the level of your expected brutality is unsustainable. You reach a point where there are very few, if any, pornography scenes that meet your level of sadism. When this happens, usually the next step is to act out your own scenarios. It is the least you can do to satisfy your craving. This is already bad enough, but there is worse in store. Again, the violence you expect amplifies with time until, if you are truly far-gone, you get to the summit of violence. The summit is death; murder. You cannot transcend this. However, your high maintenance craving for sexual violence needs to be met. It keeps growing, too. Thus, you rack up a murder count and when even that is not enough, you make the killings even grosser. With this, you reach a plateau. Regardless of how sadistic you become, there is always a way to meet it within the plateau. This attempts to explain Tsutomu's psyche.

His grandfather's death and reaction

His reaction to his grandfather's death was intense, and his family testified that he ate part of his late grandfather's ashes in an attempt to "retain something of his beloved relative within himself". (Note here that he eats his dead grandpa's ashes in an attempt to retain some of his essence within him. Tsutomu also ate a little girl's hand after he had killed her, hence the name "human Dracula". Expression by ingestion, we shall call it. The link to this one is traceable to psychology)

Tsutomu's preservation of Konno Mari's bones and clothes

The clothes and souvenirs, much like normal trophies, are reminders of his handiwork. All in all, they may show him that at least, he is worthy of something. This will be tied together at the climax of this chapter.

Tsutomu's postcards to girls' families:

The postcard adds a sense of thrill and adventure. He is daring them to challenge his deed; to unearth it via investigation. Whereas before he was an unspectacular underachiever, he is now a creator of mysteries. Mysteries that are so compelling as to deserve investigation. His low self esteem may have fuelled his crimes.

Tsutomu's elevated brutality

Tsutomu's elevated gross behavior is consistent with the pornography analysis earlier. He goes back looking for the dismembered corpse and brings them back home. Are these souvenirs perhaps? It appears he feels compelled to replenish a self esteem that has been low since his childhood days. In a way, his esteem was too seriously damaged to prop up in the normal fashion regular people do.

Tsutomu's relief over his father's death

Tsutomu's father was a symbol of his own incompetence. Now that he is dead, this is like a load off his back. Even more significant, he is dead on account of Tsutomu's "achievements". He has, according to him, slain his enemy. In this way, his ravaged esteem allows him to visualize the whole thing as a victory.

Ted Bundy: The Crazy Necrophile

Who Was Ted Bundy?

Theodore Robert "Ted" Bundy was born on November 24, 1946. He was a serial killer, kidnapper, rapist as well as necrophile who violated and killed numerous young girls during the 70s. Shortly before execution, he confessed to 30 homicides in 7 states.

Bundy's surname was Cowell, initially, and he was born to Eleanor Louise Cowell. His father's identity has never been unearthed. However, there was suspicions by some, that Louise's own violent and abusive father Sam may have sired Bundy. For the first three years of his life, he lived in his maternal grandparents' home and was led to believe that his grandparents were his parents and his mother was his older sister. However, a cousin showed him his birth certificate and called him a bastard. It was in this way that Bundy knew who his real mother was. Throughout his life, he would harbor a strong resentment toward his mother.

Bundy clearly expressed affection toward his grandfather, and spoke of "clinging to", "respecting" and "identifying with" him. However, he admitted that true to the words of others who knew his grandfather, Sam Cowell was a violent man. He was a bully who hated Blacks, Jews, Italians and Catholics and beat his wife as well as the family dog. Once, he threw Julia, Bundy's aunt, down a flight of stairs for the simple crime of oversleeping.

Even at the young age of 3, Bundy exhibited odd behavior. Julia recalls waking up from a nap one day and finding herself surrounded by knives and a 3 year old Bundy standing by her. He was smiling.

Bundy becomes "Bundy"

Up until this time, his surname was Cowell, even though his mother had changed hers to Nelson. She moved out of her parents' home and met up with Johnny Bundy whom she later married. They conceived four children of their own and Ted's surname became Bundy.

Bundy keeps distance between himself and his stepfather

Despite attempts to involve young Ted, Johnny was met with distant coldness. Ted would later complain to his girlfriend that Johnny was neither his real father nor a very smart man.

Violent pornography

Ted Bundy was addicted to violent pornography, which according to him in 1979, played a pivotal role in who he became.

Bundy's college girlfriend and his rejection

In 1967, while in the University of Washington, Bundy became romantically involved with a classmate. While her real name is not known, she went under multiple pseudonyms, the most prevalent one being Stephanie Brooks. He dropped out of college the following year and not long after, Stephanie dumped him. She cited his "lack of ambition" and "immaturity" as the reasons for her frustration with him. This probably marked the pivotal point in his life. Devastated, Bundy travelled to Colorado and then further east.

1968 to 1974

Bundy was one busy man during this period. He met up with relatives in Philadelphia and Arkansas, threw himself into political campaigns and at one point, worked as the personal assistant of Ross Davis, Chairman of the Washington State Republican Party. He enrolled in the University of Washington, this time on a Psychology major. He was well regarded by his professors. Later, he enrolled in UPS and the University of Utah for law, and strong letters of recommendation from Davis and his UW professors ensured he got through. He would hook up again in 1973 with Brooks, who marveled at his changed and serious nature. Despite dating another woman called Elisabeth at the time, he courted Brooks and even proposed marriage. Then one day, he broke off all contact with her, ignoring all her phone calls and letters. He would later say, "I just wanted to prove to myself that I could have married her."

By 1974, his class appearances had dropped drastically. He stopped attending law school altogether right about when young women began to disappear.

The first murders

Bundy gave different stories to different people of his first murders, so it is hard to pinpoint when he first started killing. He hinted at his first murder taking place in 1971, though his first documented killing is in 1974. There was strong evidence showing that he killed Annie Burr, an 8 year old girl in 1961 when he was 14, but he repeatedly denied this. By 1974, he admitted that he had mastered the necessary skills to leave minimal incriminating evidence. Note that this was an era before DNA profiling was in place.

February 1, 1974 saw Bundy commit his first documented murder, breaking into UW student Lynda Healy's basement room, beating her to a pulp and dressing her up before carrying her away. Female students would begin disappearing at the rate of one student per month.

In August of 1974, the University of Utah Law School gave him a second acceptance. He moved to Salt Lake City where he called Elisabeth often and dated at least a dozen other women. He was however exasperated by the extra intellectual edge the rest of his classmates seemed to have over him. He claimed to have been "deeply disappointed" by this. Thereafter, a new string of homicides began and continued up until he was arrested and confessed to them in August 1975.

Feigning disability

Ted Bundy's primary method of seduction in at least 90% of his homicides involved walking up to women while on crutches or in a cast and asking them for help. He would then abduct them before violating and killing them.

A psychological analysis

Bundy idolized his grandfather and spoke of connecting with him. His grandfather was a violent man and naturally, his violent traits must have rubbed off on the young Bundy.

Resentment towards his mother and women

Exposure to violent pornography may have ignited the need for violence in Bundy. In addition, Bundy seems to never have repressed the resentment he felt towards his mother after discovering her lie. It is thus plausible to assume that he fanned this fire of resentment until it magnified into an all out hatred towards women.

Being dumped by Brooks also did not make things easier. Being dumped make him lose his grip on life and he had to leave to salve his wounds. This, as earlier content shows, was perhaps the pivotal point of his life. This was the point when he may have graduated from simply hating to all out spree killing.

Compilation And Linking Of The Mental States And Tics Of These Serial Killers

Four states of the mind link all these serial killers: resentment, rejection, perception that violence is the only way and damaged self-esteem. In a way, they are all the same thing, as rejection leads to a battered esteem and violence is used as the prop up tool for it. A low self-esteem is also synonymous with resentment. Let us look closely at these three states of mind and how they can lead to one becoming a serial killer.

Resentment

This may only be described as a stewing kind of anger. It is not the explosive kind; thus, it lacks in intensity. It lasts for a long time, boiling slowly beneath the surface before erupting like a volcano. Just about all the serial killers covered here display resentfulness towards a significant person in their lives. When it explodes, the spree killing begins, as though to act as an activity that will release the pent up resentment.

Rejection

Rejection by parents, rejection by girlfriends and significant others play a pivotal role in these serial killers becoming what they become. In addition, since most of the people who rejected them were women, most of their victims were also women.

Perception that violence is the only way

Pee Wee Gaskins was groomed into violence. From a young age, he was unconsciously taught that violence was the spine of life. It is thus not hard to see why every significant outlet in his life had something to do with violence. While he initially did it to protect himself, there came a point where he did not need protecting. Yet, he could not put away the violence he had known from when he was young, so he ended up killing for sport. Violence can also be seen in Ted Bundy's life. His grandfather was violent and yet he saw him as a role model, how twisted is that?

Damaged self-esteem

For these serial killers, the only cure for a damaged self-esteem is to act out in a bid to prove yourself worthy and capable. Too bad Tsutomu chose killing sprees to prove his capability. His esteem was damaged to the point where he could not discern in a rational manner, the difference between right and wrong.

Conclusion

This book unearths that the motivations behind the actions of spree killers all lie in the brain. If the serial killers brain had been wired differently; for instance if they had a more stable upbringing, they might have ended up differently. Who knows; with the considerable charm the likes of Bundy and Knowles showed, the ability to collect material and media that Tsutomu displayed and the grit that Gaskins showed, they might have been very valuable citizens in a different world and under different circumstances. However, this does not mean that all people who have had a difficult childhood become serial killers. What I am simply trying to show is that a child's upbringing has a huge role to play in who they become.

Thank you again for purchasing this book!

I hope you have learnt quite a lot about some of the serial killers, the world has seen.

Thank you and good luck!

CPSIA information can be obtained
at www.ICGtesting.com
Printed in the USA
LVOW10s1836191117
556916LV00018B/363/P